you remind me of you

a poetry memoir
by eireann corrigan

PUSH

SCHOLASTIC INC.

NEW YORK   TORONTO   LONDON   AUCKLAND   SYDNEY

MEXICO CITY   NEW DELHI   HONG KONG   BUENOS AIRES

ISBN 0-439-29771-0

All rights reserved. Published by PUSH, an imprint of Scholastic Inc., 555 Broadway, New York, NY 10012, by arrangement with Front Street.

SCHOLASTIC and associated logos are trademarks and/or registered trademarks of Scholastic Inc.

12 11 10 9 8 7 6 5 4 3 2   2 3 4 5 6 7/0

Printed in the U.S.A.   40
First Scholastic/PUSH printing, February 2002

for Daniel,
obviously and regardless

ACKNOWLEDGMENTS

My parents are saints and my brother and sisters are their best marvels.
Thank you for your limitless love and enduring support.

Likewise, I have been spoiled by the extraordinary generosity of a battalion
of teachers. All my gratitude to Suzanne Gardinier, Barbara Herzberg,
Marie Howe, John Kendall, William Melvin Kelley, Michael Klein,
Steven Loy, Thomas Lux, Sharon Olds, and Jean Valentine.

And to those tweedy professors in the making:
Aaron Balkan, Noel Sikorski, and Jason Schneiderman.

Without David Levithan and Nancy Mercado, this book would still be
a pile of pages hidden under my bed.

Without Dina Nunziato, I would be a crazy, skinny girl
hiding under that pile of pages.

Finally and fiercely, love and gratefulness to Clay Chapman, Becky Hayes,
Hutch Hill, Eli Kaufman, Josh Powell, and David Schankula.
The secret of the clever kids is their tender hearts.

Mischief *and* On Christmas Eve, Doctor Releases Her In Time For
Midnight Mass *first appeared in the Bellevue Literary Review.*

She Tries Out for Varsity Recklessness and Only Makes JV

When you first wake up and the one good eye focuses
on my face, I only ask if you understand where you are
because that's how they handle comas on M*A*S*H — I don't expect
to see your eye travel across the white room, squint under
the long tube of fluorescent light and decide heaven. You say,
You swallowed the poison and I took the dagger and now
we're two pillars in heaven. And I put my knuckles in my
mouth and press the button that will summon the nurse.
When you say, You drank the poison and I had to follow, I argue No.
You shot yourself and almost died. You would have left me
behind and I would have been so angry. This is the hospital
where people will help you get well. And you say No. This is a
play. This is when we stand together in front of God. You look
beautiful.

Right now, I weigh eighty-four pounds. My skin is yellowing
again and each morning my hair fills the shower's drain. Later,
I will look back and wonder who let me in that room, but at this minute
I'm remembering our first date, how you told me you couldn't imagine
marrying anyone who wasn't Jewish and I told you, just as earnestly,

1

as gently, that I couldn't imagine getting through high school
without killing myself. And you said Well that gives us three years. Now
I'm wondering who let me near you in the first place, why no one noticed
me careening towards you and pulled you out of harm's way for a talk.
What was the student council president doing with the girl who ate sandwiches
at the civil war graveyard?

Back then, when you ran after me every time I tore from a room,
I saw you taking care of me. Here you are bandaged. Here you are
with your scalp stapled to your skull. Explaining you were only
following me. Later, I'll understand the chemistry of mania and
delusion. We'll blame all of this on LSD. And once I start
eating again, I'll swear I began sitting at the table again for you.
We'll promise I'll live if you live. I'll tell the story and say
I couldn't watch him working so hard towards his old self
without wanting mine back too. Couldn't watch him fighting
to recognize the alphabet only to head home and ride the treadmill
back to eighty pounds. But really, you did the thing I did other
things in place of. You slid open a cardboard box and placed
a bullet in the chamber. You found the way to hold it and then
fired. The thing I couldn't do. And rendered my smaller gestures
smaller and somewhat pointless.

Poem for Myself, on the Free Throw Line, Fifteen Years Old

Count this as the last winter you're able
to keep yourself warm.
When the buzzer sounds,
Coach will toss you
your warm-up pants, chase you
with your jacket. She'll holler
There's snow on the ground. You'll catch
your death. But you'll tuck the long sleeves
and bell-bottoms under your arms anyway,
saunter out to your mother's station wagon,
sweat steaming off your shoulders,
the frost stiffening your ponytail. Home court —
you've spent hours right here,
basket after basket, past practice,
running extra laps for air balls.
Coach calls you Killer. You're a "Big
Girl," a power forward who fouls
out every fourth quarter. You've lost
teeth on this gymnasium floor. Each night, you soak
your ankles, study history with ice packs

3

on your knees, but your legs are still
two blue ribbons of bruises. Every loose
ball has you skidding into
a new wood burn, maybe even
a bloody nose. Coach says
you're young — you'll grow into
your height, get some grace
in your game. But she doesn't train you
to guard yourself as fiercely
as your opponent down court,
as carefully as your left-hand dribble.
There's still forty pounds
between you and your future,
but they'll peel off as easily
as those snap-on trousers. You'll realize
you can steal your body
like a slow pass, sucking on single
grains of white rice, whole
coffee beans and besides
two fingers stuck down your throat
can intercept anything. So
you'll shiver through August,
return for pre-season and Coach
will ask if it's mono. A few team
meals and she'll teach you
to keep score. She'll start staying late
with the tall freshman. But right now
it's you who's poised on the red paint
like some unsprung coil. Muscles strung
under your arms like electric cables.

And you still expect every ball you sail
through the net to earn you something else,
some mysterious level of respect, maybe even
a piece of the boy slouching out of the weight room.
You haven't learned to pare yourself down yet,
to sit with your memories of strength, on the bench.
You think you can settle everything with this basket.
And you still believe you're supposed to win.

Lone Stars

We met on Texas. Not in Texas, but on
the red section of that enormous map
stretched out across the gymnasium floor. It was
a game and the whole school had been divided
into teams. Because he was on
the student council, I knew his name.
And through some shocking goodness
he knew mine. He even yelled it
when he grabbed the hat off my head
and replaced it with his own. Said it again
softly when he tugged the brim down
over my eyes. Once world peace was restored,
we watched a film strip. The whole gym
flickered, dimmed and he pulled me back
to lean against him over El Paso. In a year,
my entire planet will shrink to one locked
hallway. But right now, this boy has his hands
resting above my knees. I mean my thighs
are warm beneath a boy's hands for the first
time. The hat on my head smells like

my older brother's room and the whole world
seems possible to master, printed on
plastic, rolling out from under our feet.

First Date Poem

You invited me bowling but we didn't go bowling. Instead
my father dropped me off at your house the night before Easter
and we watched a video in your basement rec room — a movie
about mobsters and when one man cut off another man's
ear, you leaned over and loosened my ponytail. Your dog
sprawled between us on the sofa and we pet her together so that
every once in a while, I would reach over to stroke Sadie and feel your
hand beneath mine instead. And when I went upstairs to use the bathroom,
I came back to find both lamps turned off and thought this
is going to be the night I lay back and a boy unbuttons my shirt,
the night someone else besides my older sister helps me
unclasp my bra. By tomorrow morning, I'll know how hard it is
to breathe with the weight of a whole person balanced on my chest.

But none of those things happened. When the last gangster
fell to his knees on the screen, you stood quickly, as if the getaway
car sat idling in your driveway. And I followed you
across the bicycle path shadowed by poplars. Only one streetlight
lit the playground so it looked like the set of a play about two kids
who are in love and have to sneak to the school playground

to meet late at night. And it was that quiet, too — as if all the windows
glowing yellow along the street housed our hushed audience.
I stood on the swing's worn plank, held the chains, and you
pushed me so that every time I breathed in, I'd feel your hands
at the small of my back. The only other time you touched me
that night was to lift me off and set me down on the mound of sand.

At ten o'clock when she pulled into the drive, my mother asked
if I had a good time, if I thanked your parents, and when I told her
we ate pizza made from crackers called matzo, she said I
see and made me dye the Easter eggs as soon as we got home.
And my sisters and I giggled about that — me half asleep and sinking
the eggs into cups of colored water. Maureen teased Promise Daddy
you'll marry Catholic and he might let you go to sleep.
I used the white crayon to letter I love Danny K on each delicate
shell, so that every egg my family hunted for that next morning
stood for you. You — hidden in Mother's spider plant, perched
on the fireplace mantel. You — locked behind the glass of the
grandfather clock. Do you see how precious to me you were already?
My parents have a snapshot in one of the albums — I'm holding
up the basket brimming with pastel eggs, shimmering
like some ecstatic saint. Three dozen of them, with your name
spelled out in careful white print — all of my first, brittle
love for you, offered to the camera.

The Argonaut Room

I have still never seen the inside of the room
where you spent winter afternoons facedown
on the floor or on your knees with your arms
wrapped around another boy on all fours.
When those doors sprang open to let the team
stumble out, wet and creased, like clothes
from the machine, I could peer partway in and see
maroon vinyl mats lining the floor, but nothing
else — I couldn't have just wandered inside
and stood in the room's center. The girls
basketball team practiced right outside and Coach
worked us hard; we ran sprints. We ran laps and
scrimmaged until we needed to towel up the sweat
under the hoops. But every time the wrestling
team emerged from its secret northeast cavern,
the entire field house would quiet a little — you'd
all look so weary and wrung out, dragging
yourselves around the perimeters of the courts.
You'd brace yourself against the wall, waiting,
and, when it was your turn, brace yourself

against the fountain to gulp. Almost unrecognizable
in the practice singlet, the soft-soled boots, you
would never look up or grin or even nod to me
under the basket — your back turned, stooped
between two of the boys I knew you would
hurt if you could, who called you fairy and
fag in the hallways between classes. After the
whole muscular line slunk back in, the assistant
coach would shove the doors shut behind you. And
I'd hear whistles again, the tumble of bodies
against the mats and wonder what they were doing
to you in there, what they were turning you into.

He Didn't Make the
Greatest First Impression

My father doesn't dislike you because you're
Jewish. My father dislikes you because
you hurt me. Way back when I was a sophomore
still writing your name inside the cover of my
geometry book. In May, right after we first met
and I thought maybe you'd ask me to the junior
prom. My mom was already eyeing dresses and
trying out different kinds of braids in my hair. But she
was on some bus trip to Niagara Falls that weekend.
It was just me and my dad and he sat in the living
room with the newspaper while I was washing dishes
in the kitchen, on the phone with Paul Caldwell,
your friend, who later you'd argue was never
your friend, who told me I'm only telling you this
for your own good, but Dan told a bunch of us guys
that he thought you were too fat to take to the prom.
And that's when I bent over, holding on to the edge
of the kitchen sink, it hurt that badly and my father
came running in, convinced I had cut myself
on a steak knife or shattered a glass in my hand.

And I couldn't breathe enough to explain so he kept
prying my hands from my belly, checking my palms
and my shirt for blood. I'm sure he wished only
for one of my big sisters to glide in, but it was just my dad
and me that night and he did the best he could.
After I fell asleep doing sit-ups on the family room
floor, he carried me upstairs to bed and he must have been
cursing you the whole heavy trip up. And later
when they caught me hiding food, when my mom
would stand me on the scale and cry at the numbers —
Those mornings, when I would bundle up at five to run
he'd creep behind me in the station wagon in case I fell
and didn't get back up. Sometimes I'd make it
home just to faint in the shower and my dad had to
listen for that tumble and rush in to swing the faucet
from hot to cold. It didn't matter that you swore you never
said it, that instead of buying anyone a corsage, you hid
at your parents' beach house, burying empty bottles
in the sand. My dad couldn't have known that the mornings
he had to look at my naked body in the tub and anyway
he wouldn't have cared. By October, my spine was outlined
in bruises on my back with nothing to stop those bones
from rubbing against skin. Who else could he blame
for what I had done to myself? You were just a polite voice
on the telephone, always calling during supper, some snot-nosed
prep school punk. I was my father's littlest girl, his hell
on wheels, running away from him each morning,
just ahead of his headlights, around and around the block.

So She's Paid Her Dues

At your parents' house, the morning after
Yom Kippur, we wake in the room
you slept in through high school and you
stretch across the high school bed to take
an album from the high school bookcase.
I'm not in there. It's a family vacation,
the summer after we first met — I recognize
that spring's favorite shirt and the baseball
cap you wore all through sophomore year.
And finally I understand why I was so crazy
about you — There you are in every glossy
rectangle, strutting down the dusty streets
as if you knew the language. When I
was fifteen, I felt like a stranger in the 7-11
around the corner but there you are sitting
comfortably on the camel like he was your
camel. There you are with your sister thrown
over your shoulder — the handsome bandit
in the marketplace. Off the margins of the magnetic
pages, I am across the ocean sitting up

14

again and again, spitting each bite of dinner
into my parents' convenient cloth napkins.
I believe I'll move more easily through
our school's fierce halls if there is less of me
here. I'm fifteen and tired of tripping over myself,
all my papers spilling out of my book bag.
Right now, I'm sitting naked next to you
in bed with my bare breasts resting
on the album's plastic sleeves and I wish
that girl could see this, could slow down on the
stationary bicycle long enough to see how
it all turns out in the end. But she can't stop
pedaling. She still knows what we rarely let ourselves
remember these days. You have to see her
lessened before you love her. She still has years to deny
herself before I get this place in this bed.

Medical History

When did you begin to experience dramatic weight loss?
        The spring I turned sixteen, after experiencing
  a dramatic desire to lose weight.

What fueled this desire? Did you believe others considered you overweight?
        I believed others didn't consider me very often. I felt
      too much, burdensome. In the window beside my bed,
    a hole broke through the mesh screen. I used to write
   help me on scotch tape across pennies and poke
  the coins through the hole. One day I decided
 This is stupid. There are other ways
to ask for help. Thin was one of them.

How did you hope to be helped?
    Someone would take my shoulders in their hands
   and shake. They'd say Look what you're doing to yourself —
  You have so much to live for. Or they'd promise You're safe now.
No one will hurt you again.

You desired attention?
        Rescue. Attention didn't always get things done.

Do you acknowledge your life was privileged?
        I attended expensive schools. My face was pretty
      enough that men sat next to me on the train, even if other
    rows of seats were empty.

What made the weight loss dramatic?
        I left for summer camp and came home. Ten weeks
      I ate only rice, fruit, and small bites of fish. Castaway
    on an island, only it was New Jersey. At first
   everyone acted happy for me. I dressed up
  for school, tried out for the play.

At first, others seemed to approve of the dieting?
        On the first day of school, he followed me from class
      to the lockers. We signed out scripts for the play
    in the library. He took more time to look at me.
 Everyone took more time to look at me, all of a sudden, then.

Baggage

Before it ever started, before I even worried about it,
our whole family watched a Sunday night television movie
about bulimia. The girl on the screen threw up in jars
and then stacked them on her closet shelves. Her parents
had already caught her shutting herself in the bathroom
after dinner, had pried the locks from the doors. I only
started after my mom made me sit for supper with the family
again. They caught me spitting food into my cloth napkin,
so I was only allowed paper and couldn't keep it on my lap.
When I stood to wash dishes, my mother unfolded it and looked.
The dog got put out before we sat down. No more table scraps.
So I collected ziploc bags, the gallon size, and filled them.
Kept them sealed in a suitcase and slid the suitcase under my bed,
beside a duffel full of food I'd scraped from plates that summer.
When my room smelled, I snuck out at night with the spade
to bury some in the yard. I remember holding the bags of thick liquid
and imagining a full stomach, an organ being lifted from the body.
I could have carried them in a wheelbarrow to the dumpster
behind the corner pharmacy or stashed the bags in our trash cans,
the night before pickup. I don't know what the point was
of keeping them, why I needed them so close by.

It Was a Comedy

That year, they cast me in the school play
as a woman who would not eat. Each week,
the class mother who sewed our costumes
would rip out the seams of my dress,
then stitch it more tightly against me. He played
the waiter in the restaurant who fumbled
with all the plates, the full platters of meat.
Each afternoon, before rehearsal, he'd hold
open the car door for me and someone older
would drive us to the diner, a bakery, or
some deli — any shiny counter, impossibly laden
with food. It took time before I could raise my hand
and point to all I could handle. If I picked milk,
he'd pour it in the glass. If I chose bread,
he'd spread on two pats of butter. Once,
he brought back a chocolate eclair from the glass case
and we bit it at the same time, from different ends.
Afterwards, I did not disappear to kneel
in front of a toilet and that meant I loved him. Do you
see that? It used to be so easy for us to prove —
My mouth only had to close around his
spoon. He would say Taste, he'd say Try.

The Drama Club

The fourth night I sway
on stage in the school
play is the night before
I'll wait in the hospital
lobby while my parents
sign me over to the doctors.
It's also the final night of the
show, the cast party. It's at
your house and your parents
have it catered. Piles of
white plates are stacked
throughout the house.
It's hard to stand without
fainting and people keep
approaching me with
full and helpful plates.
We all know why
I have an early curfew
tonight. You're down
in the basement with your

drum set barricading you
from the rest of us.
When I finally get down
there, I can't talk to you
over the snare drum
tantrum. Before I tried out
for the play, you helped me
practice my lines, winked
while the curtain first rose.
You've sat on the library steps
for an hour watching me nibble
on a banana and when Tony
Morales called me a slut,
it was you who held
his face in the sink until he
took it back. I'm not used
to being afraid while in the same
room as you. So when my
right arm prickles and then
numbs and my chest all of a
sudden feels like it's
splintering, like inside
some man is throwing
his shoulder against a door
again and again, I stick
my hand out, across the face
of the drum, and say Please
don't tell anyone but
something's wrong
with me and you hustle

21

me into your father's office,
call my parents and wait
with your hand pressed
to my breast bone.
You promise to visit me in the
hospital and I'll be strapped
to the metal bed before I wonder
whether your mom will drive you
or you'll take the bus. Right now,
I sit in the swivel chair, watching
you summon my parents and
I'm thinking about how grown up
and wise you are, how much older
than me you are. You are six
months older. You're not even
old enough to drive.

The Menu

I wrote down everything I ate in a pocket calendar
and at first, all the listed foods wouldn't fit in the squares.
At the back, the calendar had space for the phone numbers
and birthdays of my best friends but instead I cataloged
the foods I'd let myself eat and the foods I wouldn't. By
July, the three meals fit in each square and that menu
was a basket filled with four possibilities: apples, bagels,
yogurt, cream of wheat. Each box in August only had the word
Rice written in. And the same in September: Rice. Rice.
Again in October: Rice. Then I went into the hospital
and they put the tubes in, left a chart near the bed.
A nurse recorded every bag of calories sliding in.

December 12, 1993 Dear Diary —

Some days, I decide he's coming.
Once in a while, I have a reason but usually
it's just a feeling. Last week, my mom brought
an article about the wrestling team she clipped
out of the paper. It didn't really talk about him
at all, but at the bottom, where they list the results
of each match, it said *Kaufman, D — by decision.*
And I knew that meant he won. It's his first match.
Well, not his first match, but his first victory —
He'll call it his match before he wrestles
but he'll only claim it afterwards if he wins.
He's not weird — they all do that. I'm saving
the article, not for him; his mom probably cut it out
and he'll keep it, even if he pretends it's nothing.
It's nothing really, as far as reasons go, but now
we're saving the same inky slip of paper, and no one
else just skimming through the sports section
would know how important it is. Except me.

I thought he'd come to tell me about his match.
That's the sort of reason he'd come.
He'd get to say *my match* a lot and maybe
if he told anyone else it would feel like bragging.
I can't picture him here though — everything is so clean
it's harsh. Our ward isn't supposed to look like a hospital —
We have real beds and they ask our families to bring linens
from home. Laura says it looks like college
without the sharp edges. The bulimics don't really look
sick, but the anorexics do — Even the ones who've been here
for months still have really bony faces. I don't know
what I look like. Evie, the night nurse, says I can't trust mirrors,
but I don't see people as any sort of reliable alternative.
He told me I was beautiful, the night before they took me here.
But I saw the admitting nurse write down *severely emaciated*
on my chart and Doctor showed me where he typed
Anorexia nervosa in the box left blank for a diagnosis.
So now Daniel had *his match* and I have *my diagnosis.*

I thought he would come to tell me about it — the match I mean.
So after dinner I put on real clothes and Missy braided my hair
and coiled it on top to cover my bald spot. And I put on make-up
and pulled out my algebra book so he'd see I did the same thing
all the kids in our math class did on school nights.
But by then it was seven and visiting hours had started
without him. He is the only boy who's ever stood me up.
I've been out lots of times, but our first date was the first time
any boy ever stood me up. It's not like we were supposed
to meet somewhere and he didn't show, but he was

25

supposed to call to give my dad directions to his house
and he didn't. We were just going to watch movies.
But I've always teased him about it. He says he was too
nervous — to talk to my dad, to figure out how close
to sit next to me on his parents' couch. He said
he was scared and that made it okay
because scared meant he had something to lose.

I painted my fingernails, got Evie to let me brush my teeth
again, but he still didn't come. So I watched television
in the common room with Kelly and Laura and Laura's mom
who comes to visit every night just to watch television.
At nine, when Evie let Laura's mom out the door, she asked
me if I felt *my expectations had been grounded in reality.*
And I said no, because if I said yes, she'd write it
in my chart and I'd have to talk about it tomorrow
in therapy. None of the nurses believe he's coming.
So I felt pretty dumb washing off my make-up
in front of Evie and unbraiding my hair
because that was like agreeing with them.
And when we lined up for meds, Allison asked
if my boyfriend had visited and I almost started
bawling right there but Laura punched my shoulder
and said *Relax, kid — that's what this place is.*
We're all being stood up by someone.

Cuisine

What did your diet mainly consist of?
>At first I ate fruit, white bread,
>frozen yogurt, popcorn. Fish
>sometimes. If they made me eat
>anything else at the dinner table,
>I'd go up to my bedroom and throw
>up in a ziploc bag.

And then?
>Then I couldn't eat bread. Next nixed
>fish. Could eat apples but not
>grapes. Rice. Bouillon mixed in a mug.
>One week, I ate a head of lettuce and
>a bottle of diet cola each day.

Did you believe you were overweight?
>No. I had to fold the waists of my jeans over twice.
>I could splay my fingers in the spaces between
>my ribs.

Why did you continue restricting your diet?
> The tips of my fingers were frozen blue and
> when I ran, I felt things rattle at the spaces between
> my ribs. If I stood quickly, my legs swayed or gave and my
> hair fell out and filled the brush.

How did you monitor your weight loss?
> I stood on the scale each morning
> before the toilet and after, then again
> after running. After school, I stood
> on it before dinner, after I ate
> dinner and again after I threw up. Then
> I exercised. Then I weighed myself again.

So you knew you were losing weight rapidly?
> It never felt rapid.

Eurydice Pipes Up from Bed Rest

When he finally visits, he arrives
with the meal trays. Exactly
the wrong time, on the anorexia
ward. I'm sitting at the common
table with my back to that skeptical
camera and so I'm the last to see him.
Everyone else has stopped moving.
All of us embarrassed to be caught
eating. I have waited so long
and now I just want him
to leave because he has seen me
with a fork raised, quivering.
Nurse takes him away like she would
a sharp object — with grim
determination, mild annoyance.
We go back to things. David humming
and rocking. Kelly dicing her chicken
into perfect, miniscule cubes. It's hard for me
to breathe, to keep the rice on the fork
long enough to get it in my mouth.

I am sixteen years old and the life
I was supposed to be having
was just framed in the doorway.
A boy knocking at dinnertime.
At home, I would have asked
to be excused, rushed to comb my hair.
He needs a laminated pass
to come see me, punches in a secret
combination to leave. Nurse makes him
take the paper sack he's brought
with him. For the rest of my life
I will belong to this boy and his
cupcake rescue, his white box
of bakery, the quart of whole
milk. O Orpheus of the varsity
wrestling team, with your driver's license
shiny in your pocket — you're my ticket
out of here. Come back. Salty lithium,
this intravenous currently wired
to my wrist, the insistent feeding
tubes — Everything in my world
is relentless. Except you.

She Never Claimed Reliable
Narrator Status

I sat on bed rest on the ninth floor of a hospital eight miles
from our school and thought of it as eight minutes, maybe twelve
with traffic, from him and every afternoon at five after three
imagined I felt the school bell trill and then him traveling farther
and farther away. First on the bus, then later in the old family
Volvo. Somewhere in a hospital filing cabinet are my old charts
and I'm sure you will find it listed if you search — Late afternoons
are inexplicably difficult for the patient — I snatched IV's
from my wrist, pelted plastic capsules of apple sauce against the door.
Between the hours of eight and three, I believed he could hear me
if I shrieked. Somehow he'd jolt up from the geometry slump
and come barreling to my rescue. When they stuck me for blood,
I pictured Daniel standing at the foot of the bed, ready to pin
the student nurse if she missed the vein. When they fed the tubes
through my nose, I saw him thrashing against a security guard
on his way to gather me up, away. But if I choked on the plastic
hose, spoke his name out loud, I knew he would evaporate.
They have manila files filled with misunderstanding where
someone will have noted my refusal to accept his advancing on
without me, that he went skiing and to the movies and was generally

seventeen, fumbling the healthy girls and applying for college.
But that's what made evenings and weekends so terrifying: I couldn't
picture his exact course through the school corridors, each desk
he always slid into. He could have been anywhere. In the charts,
some smartass will have recorded the exact number of times he
took up the visitor's pass from the lobby: Three. They're lying.
I'm telling you he was right there with me. He never left my side.

"Patients Should Spend Leisure Time
Mindful of Their Recovery"

One of the girls who'd been released
brought in the game on a night she came back
for family therapy. She even wrapped it
and we let Kelly, the youngest, tear off the paper.
It was called Eat It Ralph! and in the middle
of the board, this fat head stuck out, mouth
gaping. That was Ralph, wearing a dirty undershirt
with what looked like gravy around the collar
and who slightly resembled the Tuesday orderly,
who escorted us down to physical rehab. Ralph's
plastic tongue hung almost to the board and
his eyelids drooped half closed, either with bliss
or pain. If you poked your finger down his throat
you could feel the metal coil of a tiny spring.
Each player drew a card, a cartoon drawing
of a particular food: hot dog, drumstick, cupcake,
wad of fries. Plastic replicas sat in a box
like the contents of a fridge in a house
at which none of us would eat. You matched
the snack to your card and then fed Ralph,

whose elastic mouth stretched cavernous
with greed. We took turns until a taco
tripped the game's gag reflex and all the pieces
tumbled out like Thanksgiving night with the
bathroom door locked, after everyone else
has gone to sleep. We thought it was hilarious —
that the thing we'd done in secret for so long
was a game some kid would find under the tree,
that we spent hours each Thursday learning how hearts
stopped in cocktails of haywire electrolytes and
somewhere was a dad pasting on the decals
of Ralph's doomed teeth. It brought us nearer
to normal. Or tipped the rest of the world's kilter
towards our side a tiniest bit. Becky brought us
the game on Friday and Doctor confiscated it
during Monday rounds, but that weekend
we lent Ralph our tremendous appetites. Sat together
in a circle, practicing all our best tricks.

Mischief

The afternoon I got off tubes, Laura rolled me
my first joint and we smoked it in my room,
sitting cross-legged beneath the video monitor
waiting for the head nurse to hustle in. Laura said
she only wanted to get me hungry and I recited
our rehearsed line: May I please have a bag of
Cheetos and some ramen noodles? Connie actually
let us go to the vending machines, but instead
of cheese doodles and cup of soup, we got
sugarless gum. They might have been meager
but we had our triumphs. Like the crank calls
from the phone booth on the pediatrics unit.
The night before Thanksgiving, we dialed
the nurses' station and Laura told Margaret Anne
her name was Lucy, that she thought she might be
bulimic; she'd devoured two pies and the entire turkey
and was purging with a spatula. Margaret Anne
kept muttering Oh dear, Oh dear, until the operator
interrupted and asked for more quarters. Once,
we ordered six pizzas delivered to the group therapy

circle. On the day her insurance ran out, and she
was released, I sat with Laura while she packed
and she told me she and Doctor were in love
and I thought it was another joke, but months
later she slit her wrists in the outpatient waiting room,
where he sat closed in his office. Bled out right there.
Margaret Anne told us and I kept remembering
the time we bribed the reluctant pizza delivery
boy — Laura huddled in the janitor's closet, laughing
until tears hit her cheeks, asking Don't you wish
you could be there when Doctor gets them? Don't you
wish you could see the look on his face?

Privileges (for Christina)

If you are gaining weight at the acceptable pace,
(which is two and a half to three pounds a week)
and you've graduated from tubes and have no clumsy
IV to dance partner alongside you — As long as Doctor
has not secured you with restraints on bed rest,
then you can sign out at the nurses' station to the
pediatric unit's toy room to play video games. It smells
like the floor where people hook up their kidneys
to machines and because we are not innocently
sick, those nurses give us severe looks before bustling
back into the rooms of the blameless leukemia patients. But
they have Donkey Kong and Burger Time and also
that unlatched window that leads directly out
to the hospital roof. Bingo. Freebird. You watch
the door while I swing over one leg at a time, then
stand in front of the view, all the cars in the lot that can drive
home. I'll yank you through the window but don't forget
to turn back, prop it open with a cheap doll torso
on the sill so we can get back inside. Sayonara psychiatric
ward, farewell to Nurse Betsy, who believes that everyone

pacing the hallway is trying to burn off breakfast. Out here,
we run laps across the speckled asphalt until our sides stitch
with pain. Then we do sit-ups, counting aloud into the night.
There are soft patches of tar to stick in a penny for each month
we've been inside. And when we race, your gown tied
in the back billows forward and your gown tied in the front
billows back and you look like a bride or some shepherdess — lost
in all her robes. Soon you'll get nervous and say it's time
to go inside. But let's crouch together for a few more minutes
and relish that good shiver, let our teeth clatter and show off
our narrow shoulders to that wide and hulking sky. Tomorrow,
on those long sofas of group therapy, we'll both claim
we want to die. But we'll mean: Please someone convince us
to stick around. Remind us over and over that we deserve
to drink even the milk left over in the cereal bowl, to sop up
what's left on our plates with bread. Because last night, we stood
on top of fourteen floors of suffering — from the maternity
to the morgue. Hundreds of beds buckling beneath the weight
of legitimate illness, thousands of plastic sacks of donated blood —
We stood above all of it and did not leap. Neither of us even dangled
from the grainy ledge or balanced on one foot on that parapet.
Let's be honest here — we've hardly approached any edges at all.

Welterweight

The nurse who's weighed me each
weekday morning for three months finally
speaks. She says Three digits. She says
Good job. And I feel like the particular hog
who's been pointed out at the trough — valued
and equally endangered. But one hundred means
I can unfold the street clothes from that suitcase sitting
forlornly under the bed, that my mother will come in
at seven to french-braid my hair. She'll sign me out
at the nurses' station and drive me to school.
It's been three months since I've been anywhere
and I want to go to school, to put on make-up
in the girls room and sleep through geometry.
By now they've dropped me from the attendance lists —
You're the one cutting class so we can pound clay
in the art studio and dangle our feet over the canal.

You sit on the library steps and play your guitar,
your tie hung loosened around your neck — No one
issues any demerits. Everyone lets it be your holiday —

me back at school, the two of us sitting together
in the stairwell again. At noon, I drink the milkshake
and eat my first sandwich in front of you.
And you bring out a little cake in a box, stuck
with three numeral candles, like a birthday cake
for a woman turning a hundred years old.

At two you leave me sitting on the field house bleachers
and at three o'clock the coaches unroll the maroon mats
across the gymnasium floor. The wrestlers jog out
according to weight. You're seventh and you wink at me
before huddling up. Your last wrestling match and you've never
worn that varsity singlet or thrown another boy to the floor
in front of me in the stands. I have sat at the long table
four times a day for it. Returned each plastic tray to the rack
empty. Drank my juice. When they untangle you from the kid
from Kimberly Academy, the referee raises your fist.

The girls cheering beside me on the bleachers see you each
morning in math, get to see you changed for gym every day
and one of them tells me how lucky I am to miss winter
exams. But she means I am lucky to have your keys
in case I need anything from the car. That you'll find me
in the gym after the meet — your hair wet from the showers.
Everyone knows how you take care of me and everyone knows
why. And it makes me a little afraid on the way back
to the hospital. You haven't checked that I've buckled
my seat belt yet or asked me if I needed a snack. I'm not sure
a hundred pounds is such a victory — not if I have to be sturdy
from now on, not if I lose your invincible care.

She Debuts to Mixed Reviews

The first time I sit at your family's table
for Friday night supper, I'm on pass
from the hospital and still will not reach
for food on my own — So after the prayer,
when the loaf of bread travels through each
pair of hands, you tear off a piece for both
of us. And then cover a plate with sweet
potatoes and turkey, set it on the mat
in front of me. You fill your own bowl
with greens and cucumbers and remind
your indignant grandmother that you have to make
weight for your wrestling match in the morning.
Tomorrow, your coach will swaddle you
in plastic wrap anyway and you'll jog laps
around the indoor track until the last three
pounds trickle down your back. Some boys
use their fingers in their throats and some
take pills to pee but back when you first
visited the unit, you promised you'd stay
above 135. Tonight, your older sister has come home

from college to point at your meager bowl with her fork,
joking How can you stand my anorexic brother?
On a sitcom, somebody's knife might clatter
to their plate but actually your dad only stands
to push back his chair, tells her I need to see you
in the kitchen, pronto. And when you first reach for me
I unfist my fingers but it's just my wrist you're after.
And you cover the plastic bracelet with your hand.

She Turns the Tables a Little

The summer you were in the hospital, in the coma and then
out of the coma, I worked at our high school's summer day care.
Each afternoon, my mother would drive me from the school
to you and every morning the people who knew us asked me
for the update. The school receptionist and the vice-principal,
the guidance counselor and the groundskeeper. The same people
who forbid me to bring you to my senior prom flocked to the
kindergarten asking How's Danny coming along? How's
our guy? When kids from school came to visit, you sometimes
wouldn't see them and I'd walk them downstairs, explaining things
importantly. The freshman in the play with us called me from
summer camp and my mom woke me up, saying Jay's on the phone —
He's very upset and I consoled him. Do you understand how it felt
to suddenly be considered capable? I had spent the past three years
on bed rest. I wasn't even allowed to choose the percentage of fat
in my milk. I think you know what I'm talking about. You used to
bring malteds to play rehearsals, mail off the manila envelopes
with my homework assignments to the hospital each week. Your
nurses taught me to walk beside you, with one arm snaked
around your waist, scurrying between you and any hard surface

and that satisfied me. I felt useful, guarding you from the treacherous
wall. I'll admit that. But not so fast, Reverend Role Reversal — Years
before, after I finally returned to school, it was you who led me
to my classes with one hand resting on my back. You stood close enough
to whisper in my ear, close enough that I could take your arm, the way
a blind woman will take the offered arm — in debt, with relief.

Back When the Walls Had Ears

One of the boys you smoked with at lunchtime
came over to your house after school and you sent him
upstairs while you asked me. You said Cory just told me
he heard you promise you'd lose all the weight as soon as
they let you out of the hospital. And I said Cory is a
pothead who doesn't even know me. Why would I say that
out loud anyway? And you said That's not an answer.
And I said I don't know what he's talking about. So
you said Swear to me. And I swore to you and I lied.

On Christmas Eve, Doctor Releases Her in Time for Midnight Mass

My father signs each form while the long rows of family wait
at the cathedral. All the foil-wrapped packages glitter beneath the tree.
Connie has my bed linens folded in a pillowcase, meds packed
in a wax paper bag. Chewing gum, disposable razors,
the bracelet with the sharp clasp, a box of confiscated laxatives —
everything returned from the locked cupboard, neatly labeled.
Seven months of dried roses, bathrobe, slippers and pajamas,
a page torn from the Garfield coloring book with Good Luck!
I hope you beat this terrible disease!!! Love, Kelly Cabot
written across his blank pan of lasagna. The wrinkled pocket
calendar, three meals penciled into each earnest square,
the aluminum cans of nutritional supplements. Food diary.
All of it piled into the wheelchair I won't sit in. All of them
assembled at the nurses' station with a homemade card
and a plant stolen from the pediatrics unit. It's hard for us all
to embrace without envying the relief of bones on each other's backs.
I leave, pushing everything I've gathered like a frail sister in front of me.

In twelve hours, I will fill a seat at the dining room table for Christmas brunch. In fourteen, I'll kneel at the toilet with my two longest fingers reaching towards the back of my throat. And in twenty-six days, the northeast elevator will slide open again and I'll step back in, my own kind of miracle — less than I am now, less than I've been before.

Her, As Repeat Offender

Why do you think you relapsed after your first hospitalization?
        That fall, I played the lead in the high school play.
      Left and then returned in winter to star
    in the recovery follies.

You experienced the sensation of being onstage?
        All the girls ate lunch on the lawn.
       Some of them would eat the same
      foil-wrapped sandwich, bag of chips
     as always. Some would eat only
    what I did, even take the same
   number of bites from the bagel
  before tearing it to toss
 to the geese.

Were you self-conscious about your eating disorder?
        I wore sleeveless dresses
       even with scars on my wrists.

Did you expect to be readmitted to the hospital?

I used to take a taxi from school
to the outpatient clinic across
the street from the ward.
On the way, I would drink
a whole two-liter bottle
of diet cola to weigh in three
pounds heavier on the scale.
I stuck batteries in my
underpants and taped
the weights from the
cuckoo clock under
my arms.

So you were deceiving your doctors?

It takes a lot to drink that much
carbonated water. An effort. That's
as much as I could do and I
did it.

You felt helpless to relapse?

Each day the cab eventually parked
at the clinic's curb. It was inevitable but
not the only thing. I could be
inevitable too.

Between the Sex and the
Rock and Roll

It's difficult to picture myself at sixteen and think I was anything
spectacular. Hard to reason that because I disappeared into the hospital,
he suddenly started stashing rolling papers, plastic baggies of weed
in his backpack. The first time we sat at the river he said he'd tried it
once. Proudly. But he also claimed he was only a virgin
by choice so I thought it was that kind of bravado. I looked
impressed because I wanted his hand up my shirt. I didn't feel like much
next to him, worth him. So it's strange to look back and realize
that his eyes didn't glaze over so often until they saw me shut in with tutors
and tube feedings. That I left first. Stopped eating, really meaning
to die. And slowly so that everyone had to stand by and watch.
I would have locked my mother in stocks like some colonial criminal
just to make her see me. I'm saying I meant real harm. But not
to him. By the time I came back to school, all those girls
who'd shunned me made room at their table at lunch. Everyone
wanted to watch me eat. And he'd made his own name for himself.
Lines of coke at Jordan Grafman's house, between laps in the pool.
Hours spent deciphering Doors' lyrics, acid melting on his tongue. Or
on slow days, just him closed alone in his car with windows rolled up —
licking the papers like an expert, tapping ash from the pipe's screen.

He Tries Out the Concept of
Tough Love

I'm standing at the phone booth
on the eating disorder unit with
quarters piled on the counter. Back
in the gown, so I have one hand
pinching it closed, one hand slotting
coins, the phone cradled between
my shoulder and ear. This is not
allowed. I have another eight
minutes before the orderly delivers
the dinner trays and the second shift
of nurses pours out of their station.
In the first week, the patient is confined
to the room. No visitors or telephone
privileges. Interaction with other patients?
Limited. Yesterday, I took a taxi from school
to the outpatient center. Doctor set me up
on the scale and then would not
let me go home. Now I want to pull a pair
of pantyhose over my face and spray
the group therapy session with bullets.

I'll stand hostages in front of the windows
and wait to hear your voice blare
from the police bullhorn. It takes six
quarters to reach your area code. I want
a ride home. I want a place to stay.
You sound like you've practiced
when you say It seems to me
you weren't ready to come home
or else you would have worked
harder to stay. And you tell me
you have a chemistry lab to do,
your mom needs the table set for supper.

The New Girl

We knew she was coming because sometime after weigh-in and
before breakfast, Margaret Anne had carefully spelled her name
out on the patient blackboard: Heather. There were three of them
in outpatient and it could have been the one who also cut herself or
the one we all liked — the redhead who smuggled in sweet
and low packets and cold cans of diet cola, but most likely it was
the third Heather, who had not been doing so well, who did nothing
in group session besides shrug and weep, who wore deep,
V-necked sweaters and had a clavicle we all coveted. Probably it was that
Heather so all the smallest girls started pacing the corridors and scratching
at their scalps. And we grilled Margaret Anne at the meal table
but through the entire bleak effort of sausage and cereal, she wouldn't tell.
Saturday morning and nothing to do but watch cartoons, dread lunch,
and wait for the new girl. At noon, orderlies wheeled in the stack of trays
but no gurney, no wheelchair even. Then kitchen had sent up her first meal
but we left it on the rack — tuna sandwich, carrot sticks, saltines, pint of milk.
Canned pears left to languish in their own syrup. Three o'clock meds,
then those of us with garden privileges paraded down, ran covert
laps around the roses, pocketed sugarless gum from the lobby gift shop.
We came back to find Margaret Anne gone and Connie on 3 to 11. She

53

made us play checkers and when Missy asked who would take Bed Nine,
she said Mind your own bizness bony — someone as crazy as you.
During dinner Doctor strode in with the treatment team,
called Connie and drew the blinds in the nurses' station. A wad of gum
on the video monitor then a riot of illicit activity —
Laura tumbling egg noodles into her boot, spilled juice,
my chocolate pudding sunk under the potted rubber tree.
Eleven pats of butter smeared beneath our chairs. And then
nothing. No storming nurses armed with liquid supplements,
no avenging milkshake brigade. Only the grim team, clutching kleenex
and a floor meeting declared. Just Connie erasing Heather's name
off the board and then a gathering silence.
And somehow we knew that meant she'd died and figured
she'd done it herself. Allison, who wasn't allowed cutlery anymore
and Gary, who watched the girls change on the nurses' monitor, David,
who only wore soccer cleats and stood at the locked door, kicking visitors,
Laura and Kelly and Missy and me — all of us knew even before Doctor
called it an accident. And while the nurses started pulling files to fill Bed Nine,
Alex boosted me up to the bookcase and I went to work on the sticky camera.
O, one-eyed god of mercy, help. Nobody wants to move into our neighborhood.

Summer of 1995

The way I have heard it, your sister drove you home
from the doctor's and then asked you to walk the dog.
While good Sadie led you down the street and back,
your mother called mid-flight en route from California
to New York. And when you came in again and bent
to unclip the leash from the collar, your sister said
Mom's on the phone and you said nothing. You only
closed the cellar door behind you as you went down.
Then they heard a noise which, to your mother on the phone,
might have sounded like one burner on a gas stove igniting or
a truck backfiring streets and streets away. Your mother said
Check and so your sister checked and found you bleeding
with the gun in your lap. And for the next two hours,
your mother sat on the plane with a policeman on the line
tethering her to earth. I was at a garden party with my new
boyfriend. He was teaching me to make torches out of cattails
and kerosene and the corsage he'd brought me covered
the scars on my wrist. It was July and I was pushing away
plates again, swallowing those fast black pills but
I remember smiling at Ben, buckled into his hotshot car

and thinking I hadn't smiled like that at any boy since you.
I used to believe that any harm that came to you would visit me
also — a sudden crippling pain, an eclipse of brightening light.
But I felt nothing. And the next day, Ben and I spread
the local paper out on my kitchen table, looking
for the movie listings and a slim column on the front page
rose up: North Brunswick Man Shot and I only
stopped to read it because that's where you lived —
in the sprawling neighborhood as secure and tended as a tiny
national park and then I read your address and then
your name and I did not understand who was screaming
until my father covered my mouth with his hand. The next
autumn, Ben would say good-bye and drive the little red car
into a tree and my father would do the same thing
with his big hand until I bit his palm. But that
July it was you and I wouldn't let another man touch me
besides my father until I knew you would live. My mom
ushered Ben out the door, saying sorry things.
And in the morning, I sat at the hospital between your two
hoarse sisters and saw your mother, the judge, in the corner
with her hands tangled in her hair. Oh, Daniel — by the time you can
hold a spoon again, everyone who knows you will have become
meeker. And you'll peer in the mirror at your new,
uneven face, believing that you are that only one changed.

Her Alibi

Where were you the evening he sat on the cellar floor
with the gun in his lap?

     Riding in the passenger seat
      of another boy's car, turning the orchid
    around and around my wrist.

And for the first four hours of surgery?

    The party was outside and we danced
     on the patio. Torches blazed along the porch railing
and the water in my glass tasted like citronella candles.

Did you hear a shot fired?

                Nothing. Crickets. The AM radio crooning.

Were you present in the basement the evening he sat
with the gun in his lap?

     I was on my way to a garden party
      and then I arrived. Then I was dancing.

Were you satisfied with your life?
        It was unexpectedly cold. I wore
     a backless dress and wished I'd brought along a sweater.
 Shivered.

Were you hopeful?
   I hoped that someone would let me die.
  On my wrist, the freshest cut under the corsage
was seeping into the flower. That satisfied me.

Did you ever share this wish to die with anyone?
                        I did, once. I told him.

Do you remember where? Where did you tell him?
    We were sitting on the floor. Or
   I sat on the sofa and he knelt with his hands
  propped on my legs. When I said it, his hands
tightened around my kneecaps and that tickled.

And this was where?
        This was in the basement.

Mechanics

When the paramedics buckled your head to the board, your eyes still looked.
You spoke like a man who had only fallen and hit his head on the hearth. Man
sunk in an underground pipe, calling out to the helping crew. The surgeons
explained it to your parents and your parents explained it to me — how
the bullet entered between the eyes and ricocheted off the top of the skull.
Exited out below the right socket and missed most precious matter. I can
close my eyes and see the gun drop soundlessly to the carpet and then
your hand feeling for the back of your head, finding it, shockingly, intact.
Let's say it was the sudden desire for breath and light that disoriented you.
The hanging feet kicking to relocate the stool. Except I was in the chair
dragged beside your bed when you woke again. My hands on the white
blanket. I saw you see again, how your eyes widened with —   it wasn't
gratitude. Meaning: it might have been disbelief. It may have been terror.

The Rescue Squad

So you weren't the only one riding the ambulance that July. All
over the county, each night, men in scoutish uniforms heaved
the gurneys into squad rigs and went. They sat around tables
watching the ball game until the walkie-talkies squealed
from the holsters or something vibrated at their hips. They
sipped ginger ale or iced tea and waited for chest pains,
a three-car pile-up or the boy filing down the cellar steps
to press a pistol to his own face. Otherwise, they spent all night
playing hearts, they goofed off — They froze water in latex gloves
and floated them in the pitcher of lemonade. In Far Hills, men
like them lifted a boy out from under his tangled motorcycle
and had to cut away his charred blue jeans and later that boy
took the bed beside yours on the brain trauma unit. His
name was Scott and he only had a mattress since he'd swung
a chair at the fiancée he didn't recognize. And in Virginia,
the paramedics fastened the actor to a backboard after he
was thrown from a horse and so Superman was all the robust assistants
in the physical rehab room talked about. They'd have your leg
laced into its brace and you propped up against a rolling walker
and they'd say Man, you're one lucky SOB, Superman can't even breathe

on his own now — do you know that? Man, you could take down
Superman. All over the country people were being rescued or
they were not. Remember that August? I would sit on your bed and hold
the guitar while you strummed and later you'd hold it yourself
and sing. Outside, Scott's girlfriend would stare in at him
through the door's mesh window and press the stone on her left
hand into her right palm. Some of the rookies on the squad can't stand
the shifts they spend shuffling playing cards all night long.
That night, one of them drove the rig back, coasting down the slick road
of adrenaline, after he saved your life. And each time you eased open
your eyes that summer and pronounced my name, I felt blessed. Where
are you? Whom did you reach for this morning? Do you know I saw Superman
on TV last week, giving a speech in a tuxedo and his wheelchair?
He looked good — he looked ready and strong.

Her Motive

When did you first visit him in the hospital?
      Three days after. The walls of his room
      were glass on three sides. An exhibit of a man
      kept alive beneath machines. Plexiglass.
    The bandages around his head were wet,
but not red.

Did his family appear glad to see you? Did you feel welcome?
      I felt weakened. I was smallest then,
    and small enough that people stared.

His family stared?
    His family looked away. His sister led me
   to the room and spoke to the floor tiles instead of me.
  His father put his hands on my shoulders and I felt
ashamed.

Ashamed of what exactly?
    I knew exactly what my shoulders felt like.

After the initial visit, how often did you return to the hospital?
      Every day that summer. Then they moved him
      to another hospital and every day there.

Did it alarm you to see him in the hospital?
      Around the corner from my house,
        we had a firehouse. The whistle blew each day
      at six o'clock. Shrill enough that the china shook
      on the dining room hutch. That summer,
    I heard the whistle all day.

How did it feel to see him beneath the machines?
      It relieved me to see his chest work
      to lift the sheet. I could hold my hand
    near his mouth and feel breath and then
    grateful.

You felt grateful to see him in the hospital?
      At home, the floorboards shook like it was six o'clock
      constantly and our town signal was someone
      shrieking his name. It was unexpected and difficult
      to believe he had lived. I felt grateful to keep watch
    in the quiet glass room.

Did you consider yourself a grateful person?
      I used to hold an electric iron to my arm until
      the skin crackled and opened. I refused food
    until it hurt strangers to look.

And that satisfied you?

Until his father placed his hands on my shoulders.

At which point you felt?

I already told you. At which point I felt ashamed.

She Gives Him the Update

At the foot of your bed, they have a clipboard dangled
from a chain and each time a surgeon strides in, he
scribbles on it. Each doctor jots something down — the
anesthesiologist, the neurologist. And every other
hour a nurse arrives to record the digits blinking
on the machine screens, switch the IV bags, or replace
your bandages. When I finally get to see you, I need
to check the name on the chart to make sure. They
have your eyes sewn closed — blackened sockets bookend
your bruised nose. Top third of your head wears a sturdy
turban of gauze and your cheeks and chin sport a mysterious
layer of whiskers. Three years ago, your voice cracked
in algebra class — Since when have you been able
to grow a beard?   I know you can hear me.
Some people wake from comas and remember circling
above doctors working busily on their bodies. How much
have you been watching? Earlier this morning, your brother
read aloud from one of his computer textbooks at your bedside
and ran out triumphant, shouting Daniel gave me the finger!
The whole packed waiting room swayed and cheered.

Evidence

For days they've called it self-inflicted but
I need evidence. And when they finally let me
near you I bend to smell for gunpowder
on your hands. Nothing I recognize. Once
you led me down the cement cellar steps
and I thought you'd finally press yourself
to me and, openmouthed, lean in. Instead
you had set up a card table in the basement
spread with knives and cakes of unwrapped
soap. We sat on folding chairs, carving shapes and
animals. You bought the green kind for the name
Irish Spring. Afterwards, we drove back
to the hospital and the glass doors sealed me in.
Even days later, I had soap slivered under
my fingernails — My hands smelled of lemon
and lanolin, glycerin and lye.

Her Red Herring

When did you begin to see improvement in your health?
  He'd go days without speaking to
  anyone, then switch on the light
  only to see me.

And you began to feel stronger?
  I liked to put the straw between his lips,
  read magazines to him and hang the pictures
  where he could see them.

Were you under a physician's care at this time?
  The last time they put me on a scale, they also
  brought out the clipboard, all the blanks
  for me to sign myself in. He hadn't woken up
  yet. I kept staring at Doctor's lamp, thinking how
  that lightbulb might last longer. We might lose
  him before the blister on my wrist healed.

And so you were once again admitted to the hospital?
    It was a different hospital, across town
      from his. I turned eighteen then,
     allowed to choose. He was in
    intensive care.

Are you saying you refused hospitalization?
    I refused to speak
     to any of them. He would
     turn on the light only
    to see me.

Yet your health improved with no medical supervision?
     I woke up early to bend over
      Mother's cookbooks. My first time
      over the skillet for a man. Wrapped
     the plates in tinfoil, then in towels
    to keep warm. If I packed myself
    yogurt instead, he scowled.
   Made me show him
the bottom of the cup.

And your progress corresponded with his?
    When he was strong enough, we took
    him to a deli. He rested his knees
   against mine and crumbled
crackers into my soup.

Did you ever discuss your health with him?

      Once he made me tell him the worst thing
    that ever happened to me. I saw the leg brace
   and the map of surgery on his scalp. Idiot.
  I said, "This is the worst thing."

To happen to you?

    To him. This was the worst thing to happen to him.

Incentives

Some afternoons, when you would not sit up
in bed or change out of the black t-shirt or
speak to the woman at your bedside with the
clipboard, your parents would bring your dog
to the hospital gardens and we would wheel you
to the window to see steadfast Sadie, retrieving
the tennis ball like always. Two years before that,
when I had those very last pounds to gain, before
the hospital doors would spring open and spill me
back into high school wilderness, my mother left
my prom gown hanging from the IV stand.
Every time I stalked to the common room for a
meal, I had to push it aside. And during my freshman
year at college, you used to call from the halfway
house and we'd spend hours declaring telephone
love — Those afternoon acquittals when you'd swear
no one could have prevented your pulled trigger
and I'd promise I had never seen your eyes glint
in the blue digitals of the electronic scale.

My dorm would empty for dinner and in your city,
the addicts in adjacent apartments would turn on
their televisions and by the time our rooms darkened
around us, our throats sounded sore from talking. Once
you asked me what color underwear I had on. Mumbled it so
sheepishly and I whispered back Blue, electrified
by how frequently you'd picture it — after curfew,
counting down days in the blank calendar dark.

Snapshots in the Blank Album

     And here is the spectacle of the two of us
launching sailboats in that pond behind the hospital: the lurch and stutter
of you, my narrow, haggard shiver. Crouched on the pebbled shore,
here I am propping you upright or here's you hovered between feeble me
and the August wind. Here is the leg brace in the corner and me, asleep
in a cot beside your bed. Here is how the nurses taught me to walk
beside you: with one arm snaked around your waist, shuffling between you
and any hard surface. Still. Me perched on the sill of my college dorm room,
offering. And your hands shaking then like they did when you first tried
to hold a pencil again. Once I had to tie your shoelaces — now it's my dress
you're determined to unbutton. Then the hammock at the sea. And then
the dune grasses. The splintered dock, the glittering bay. Here is your room
with the grim radiator and mine with the wooden shutters, the stained glass.
Here I am leaning against you in the bath, the bar of almond soap
 in your hand.

     And years before that. Here we are
at the river behind the school playing fields, in the darkened auditorium.
My voice evacuating its box, retreating into my body's new economy.
You, spooning soup towards me with one hand, buttering my crackers

with the other. And sitting under that mahogany table — your solemn
voice hushing the library. Here are my letters to you from the locked ward.
And you, counting off the sick abacus of my rib cage — Before, after. You
turning over my wrists in the shower. Here are those scars growing crimson
in steam. Here is the guilt distillery, functioning at maximum capacity.

Here you are sitting in the basement with the gun
pressed between your eyes. Those two blue villages,
impoverished, empty. Here, the narrow newspaper column
and here I am falling backwards into my father's arms. You, trembling
under all the engines of your recovery. But here you are alive
and so I am buckling under an endless thankfulness. Then a sudden
stunning hunger. The bells in your eyes ring and recognize.
Then there I am — the grateful girl at the head of the bread line
in this country where only your hands are dusty with flour.

She Puts the Only Witness
on the Stand

That morning, the white jacket parliament elects me
to ask about the gun. To mention it casually, but I can hardly
fit my mouth around the word. And you're not even able
to turn your head away. Ambush. Your weakened legs
and your voice croaking *Sorry. Sorry.* Hold my face
in your hands and look, criminal. Here I am in the school play.
Here I am at your senior prom. Here I am at your bedside, becoming
ransom. What belongs to you. And would you live for it?
Your hands sift through my hair and I want to think
you are thankful. The bed curtains drawn around us — this small
chapel of promises. Turned interrogation room. Outside, the suicide
sentinel paces the tiles of long corridor. Here I am holding up
a series of mirrors, some pointless police lineup. They found you
bleeding and you handed over that revolver, pleading *Finish it.* Woke
later, pinned under all this tiring equipment, all inflicted breath and beat
and now when I tell you I am only grateful for your life, you say no,
you meant sorry for the pistol's narrow barrel, its single shot.
You in the bed, wishing you'd fired twice
and me, Inspector Reluctant, grilling. My failed
assassin, my risen boy. Tears and my fist knocking on your chest.
Your one good eye, widening. Then me in that hollow
elevator — the steel heart's seal, the steel heart's plummet.

She Stands Corrected

Years after we first argued, we really
argue and I ride a bus out to Princeton
to see to our high school English teacher.
I weep in her kitchen while she shows me
how to make cucumber soup. She directed us
in the school play, visited me in the hospital, then
visited you in a different hospital. She used to
make you promise to make me eat. It always
amazed me, how determined you were to take
care of me, chasing me out of the cafeteria
with a carton of juice. A magnet holds
a photograph of you, in costume, to her
refrigerator door and she'll send it home
with me, between the pages of a borrowed
book. She says "It's easy enough to mistake
being grateful for being in love." And I
say "No, he's never been grateful like that.
He hates that I was there at his bedside
before he woke up." She pours the green
soup into the bowl and gives me a spoon.
She brushes my hair behind my ears and
tells me "I wasn't talking about him."

Track Conditions

After you decide again that every fortune
unfurled from a cookie means me and I decide
that every song on the jukebox means you,
I travel from college to see you in your first
new apartment. Save thirty dollars taking the train
first from the city to Trenton, then from Trenton
to Philadelphia. Four hours to shuttle eighty miles.
And somewhere on the way out of Jersey,
that first train trembles and slides into a long,
screaming skid. Lights falter off and the bags
on the overhead racks hit the floor. The man
across from me surrenders his handkerchief
to the woman behind him with the nosebleed
and the mother in front of me unbuckles her baby
from his stroller to take him in her arms and
Mr. Handkerchief says That's not safe —
Leave the kid in the carriage. And she says Who
do you think you are? And we sit bickering in dark
panic until the man who collected our tickets
picks his way through the aisle. He has a flashlight
and calls us folks. He says Folks, please keep calm.
And I notice he calls the person we hit

76

an unfortunate soul. He says An unfortunate soul
stepped out on to the tracks and our brakeman
did not have enough warning to stop. For some
reason, I want to turn to that woman
with the nosebleed and say If the paramedics
had given up, then the boy I'm going to visit would count
as an unfortunate soul. But then the fluorescent lights
choke on and that ticket collector speaks again,
says Folks, a member of our crew is understandably
distraught. We'll wait just a few minutes for relief
to arrive from the next station. And I wonder
if the shaken brakeman will lower himself
into a passenger seat and ride, staring out the window.
Or maybe the jeep that delivers his replacement
will ferry him home. He'll sit with his head
across his wife's lap and bunch her skirt in his fists,
the way you have mine those nights you've said prayers
before unbuttoning my dress. Who do you think
I am? By the time we arrive in Trenton,
I've missed my connection, am already an hour and
a half late and when that train to Philadelphia staggers
to a stop, I already know the news the conductor will crackle
over the intercom, just like when the girl who told me
you'd pulled the trigger, when that same girl telephoned again
one year later, I knew she'd say something I didn't want
to know. Tonight, I sit on the second train as quietly as I sat
at Ben's funeral, worried that someone might recognize me
as the one common thread. Ben took me out the night
you held a gun to your head and fired. I knew he loved me
because he'd drive me to the hospital and sit in his car

77

while I sat by your bed. It takes more than an hour
for the police to arrive and clear the tracks ahead of our train.
It's a Friday night in May, warm enough to wait on the platform
without a jacket and two men in two states have stepped into
the brightening lights as decisively as you'd step off
a highrise. What are the statistical chances of all this?
This time the whole stoic crew stays on and the electricity
didn't even flicker. How can one death cause less of anything?
At first, when that girl called, all I could be was grateful
that she wasn't calling with news of you. Who could
forgive me for that? My father carried me out of my dorm
and that night, I dialed your telephone number at college
and said Daniel shot himself in the head. And you said
What? And I said Ben drove his car into a tree. And
when I told you it meant that there was something I
must have done to both of you, you asked Who do you think
you are? Right now I am dizzy — I want to close my eyes
against you and bite the collar of your shirt. By the time
I arrive at the station, you've given up waiting on those benches.
I describe you at the window and the man there remembers
you perfectly. He tells me you had him call my name over
and over the loud speaker. He says He was so disappointed —
he thinks you changed your mind. It's almost midnight.
I can't tell you why the whole trip took seven hours
or you'll end up on your knees, weeping into me for
your own good fortune, for those men and their dismal
lack of miracles. So when the taxi finally delivers me
to your drive, you are angry but less angry
than you'll be later on in our lives, worried but less
worried than you have been before. Now I remember

how you held my face in your hands that night — like
it was a face you had stapled a sketch of on every
telephone pole across the city. And now, when we kneel, each
at our separate beds, we thank and pray for other things.
Who do we think we are? In my mind, the brakeman walks away
from the train into that darkened tunnel, his head
bent down, his cap in his hands.

Her Motivation

And your increase in weight that summer did not cause you concern?
     It was weeks before he opened his eyes.
     I'd sit at the table and picture him in the metal
    apparatus of the bed, the bed rising
   up. Imagined fastening a thick cord to
  the rail and tugging to keep it tethered,
 like on a kite.

You believed he might just float away?
    Maybe a rabid dog.
   On a leash. I needed to be
heavier to anchor him down.

Did he behave irrationally; was his "head in the clouds"?
     His head was wrapped in gauze. Sometimes he sat up in bed
    and talked about the school play, the prom. Sometimes
   he claimed the scar along his thigh indicated he was
  actually the biblical figure of Jacob.

Jacob, the brother of Esau?
    Jacob, who wrestled God's angel and lived.

And who represented the angel in this scenario, do you think?
      I assumed that when he said angel
    he meant gun.

Never you? He never implied that the angel stood for you?
      Later, he said that.
    I got to be the angel
  later on.

July Fourth, 1996

Two timid hours in your mother's convertible,
wedged between your sisters, my hair ropy
with salt air and whipping my face. Everyone
wants to know about college, but I'm convinced
that if my mouth opens the slightest, I'll blurt out
all the details of your naked body against mine.
The long bridge takes us out to you and you bend
to kiss me in the car, before your mother even
frees the key from the ignition. Bend to lift me
straight from the backseat, laughing at the eight
raised eyebrows. And then we sit on the porch,
surrounded by your family's clamor. I'm that pair
of silent saucer eyes peeking from the hammock,
hiding my smile in a glass of iced tea.

She Remembers the
Tearful Farewell Scene

For weeks now, my mother has been stacking linens
and sweaters in piles on the sofa. I've gained
eighteen pounds in the past two months and the small
square refrigerator already sits in the car's trunk,
smugly. But the surgeons have just reopened
your stitches and I don't know how to tell you
I'm leaving for college. If you had a bowl
of porridge cooling on the nightstand, I'd think
we were on the set of a play about the infirmary
of a boarding school. Cots of abandoned
boys and their terse and hurried nurses.

I miss your old room with the guitar
in the corner, the curtain I could tug
around us for privacy. They've shaved
the top of your head again and the staples
are back in place along your scalp.
And I tell you like it's no big deal. I'll just
see you on weekends and you grab
a hank of hair and yank my face closer,

then remember to be gentle and pet
me a little, sighing College Girl.

When I ask you for advice, I mean
I promise not to baffle my brain
with acid like you. I promise to come home
intact. Your whole mouth works to form
the words you want before you manage
to pronounce: egg crate. And then louder:
egg crate. Again, agitated — egg crate. It takes
the sternest nurse to settle you back against the sheets,
to explain you mean the orthopedic foam between
the mattress and your back. She says
You can pick one up at Caldors. Looks down
at you and adds He's been sleeping much better
with his. And you tug a few strands of my hair
again, nodding triumphantly. And I say Sure
thing. And I tell you Good-bye.

Remembrance Day

I was sitting at the desk
in my freshman dorm room
and it was April. My nineteenth
birthday had passed and
my party was without you,
piñata. You were strung up
in rehab, being tapped with the
answer stick. But you telephoned me
six days later, on the eighteenth, which
was Holocaust Remembrance Day.
I had spent the evening wide-eyed
in the lecture hall, listening to how
someone like me might hand someone
like you to the Germans for a new pair
of leather boots. I sat there thinking
I would never trade him for a pair
of boots and that said nothing so I
made it bigger: I would walk barefoot
across glass rather than hand him
over. Then it became: I would walk

barefoot across glass and then wade
through vinegar. And it was as if
I'd finally worded a spell
properly. I got back to my dorm room
and picked up the ringing phone
and you wanted answers. Why
I'd visited you every day that summer.
Why I brought presents. And I told you
that once you climbed the sterile
steps to visit me — I was still
grateful. But you asked Why else?
And I said Dear Can of Worms,
You don't know what you're getting
into. The first time I told you I loved you,
I was holding your hand through the metal
hospital railing but the first time you
heard me, I was sitting in my room,
my feet propped up on the desk. And you said
First off, I love you too. I didn't think of you
as sick and vulnerable. I thought it proved
that you were finally well. That the whole
outstretched world had recovered. And the joy
in that room? I believed it was earned.

Eventually, They Had a Sex Life

Once, years ago, at a concert, I spun around
and you had vanished — left me standing
in the middle of the stadium, my voice raw
with your name. I spent the next forty minutes
scanning each seat, chasing green jackets until I saw
you tearing through the crowd, blue eyes wild, fists
in your hair and I thought Who is he looking for
so desperately? By the time I believed you
loved me, you no longer loved me. The morning
of that concert? I woke up and swore no more
sex — for various reasons you didn't deserve
to see me naked again. But you pulled into
the driveway and, in minutes, had me stretched
across the living room sofa, my clothes tossed
on my father's reclining chair. The first time
you kissed me was the same afternoon I
leaned against the dorm windowsill, offering you
all of it. Then every button of my dress
fell through its placket. At first, our teeth
scraped against each other and I worried

we might make that noise the whole time —
banging into each other like forks in a slammed
drawer. I don't know how I ever managed
to forget how your voice shook on the phone,
taking down directions to my dorm, how you
knelt there above me with my dress in your hands,
how at first you just sat back and looked.

Homestead

At the farmers market across the road
from your college, we share a rickety table
with an old-timer, who calls me Sweet Pea,
who says You mean to tell me you rode
that bus all the way up from Jersey
to see this turkey? He'd better write
long letters home. And while the man
talks town history, you construct
my sandwich out of old habit. I sit
with my elbows on the table like a kid
letting his mom cut his meat. The man
draws a map on the wood tabletop with his
knife, marks the grocery and the college
and then a few inches away, sets down
his pint of milk and says That's my house —
a few miles down the road. Built it on leave
from Fort Dix and the wife wouldn't even
wear her ring until I put up the frame. He points
the knife at me and says You make sure he digs you
a cellar before you even say yes. These days,

folks buy houses assembled from kits, but
our boys took their first steps on floor I laid down
with my bare hands. The man makes you touch
his callused palms and when he rises from the table,
he sets down bills for our lunch too. For the rest
of this visit, I'll catch you studying your own
hands — You'll keep interrupting yourself
to remind me — That man built his house
with his own hands. And tonight, you'll rub
the hem of my nightgown between your fingertips
and thumbs and promise me two bedrooms
and a fireplace, a staircase and a banister and I will
reach for you like I have always reached for you —
as if the bed was something you'd hammered together,
as if the roof was a shelter you'd raised above our heads.

She Remembers When
He Gave Concerts

He used to set the telephone receiver down
on the floor, hook the wire harmonic trap
around his neck, duck under the guitar
strap, and call out Can you hear me?
I would holler back Yes, yes I can hear you
and picture my voice squeaking from the receiver.
Sometimes, I'd hear him sigh and then
the odd chord of the guitar tossed to the bed
right before he'd pick up the phone again and ask
Can't you hear me? And I'd say Yes, Yes
I can hear you. Then he'd set me back down,
pick back up his guitar and strum. He'd sing
the song he'd just learned that morning or
the one that meant me that day and I'd sit,
crushing my ear with the telephone, listening.
When we started it, he was still in the hospital
and I was in college. Later, he sang from the
rehabilitation center and from the halfway house.
Then he was at his college and I was at mine.
He's done it from the apartment in Philadelphia

and sang to me while I filed in the tiny cubicle
at the publishing office. He's done it from the
basement in his parents' house and from the room
he slept in, growing up. Once he went silent in the
middle of Springsteen because his father opened
his bedroom door and stared. And when
I'd call him at college and hear the shrill giggle
of another girl in his room, he'd call back later to say
Look, it's not like I'd sing to her over the telephone.
And that counted as enough, back then. You can't
decide how someone will go about loving you.
He'd finish the fourth or fifth song and then
make himself stop, telling me People would think
the two of us were crazy if they knew about this.
People would think we were insane.

They Consider Their Place
in the Gene Pool

The valedictorian of your graduating class asked the girl
who was valedictorian the year before to marry him.
We lay in my dorm room, naked in the twin beds we'd shoved
together. You left your palm resting across my belly, telling me
about the ring he'd shown you. I couldn't help it — It stung
to think of people who went to the prom with us moving on
with their lives, while you still stuttered a little, while my body
still couldn't handle donating blood. You told your mom
that night at the dinner table and she predicted Julie and Anthony
would have remarkably smart children. And so you asked her
what kind of kids we would contribute to the world and the gravy
boat in her hands stopped pouring for a moment, while she decided
they would be beautiful children and said so, not unkindly.

He Asks Her How Long She Has
Pictured Their Children

Since you first leaned against the field house bleachers
and asked me to have lunch with you, our river
picnic behind the tennis courts — the two of us just
two blue wool blazers shining right out of prep school.
Since we raced across the footbridge, skipped stones and
class, back when you'd only smoked weed once and I'd never
poked my fingers down my throat. Since you climbed that sugar
magnolia and called down *Look at me* — *Arrogance is unavoidable.*
And I did look up and of course I believed you. Since I was fifteen,
watching movies in your basement with the dog sitting between us,
both lamps turned off and your father's heavy footsteps overhead.
Since I was home and hurt on prom night, because I wore no Star of
David necklace because I was Catholic and clumsy and had
that awful haircut. Since the summer of my grim resolve
and then the dimming autumn, when my hands went blue
with cold and my closet — foul, full of hidden food. The two leads
in the high school play are arguing about milkshakes
again. We're circling the McDonald's parking lot because you feel
responsible. Since that last curtain and the cast party at your house
when you stayed in the basement behind your drum set

all night, pounding because the very next morning I was leaving
for the hospital and I stood in front of you to say good-bye
and you would not look up. All I heard were cymbals.
Since you ran after me, like always and were the only one
to hug me and you made me bring my roses and you promised
you would visit. When I kept tearing out the IV, they wheeled in
the feeding tubes and put me on bed rest. When I still
would not eat, they brought out the anatomy charts, all
their books of numbers and showed me the order of organs shutting
down and I ate first for the sake of babies; I could see them
hovering against the ceiling — all those blue accusing eyes, yours.
And those two slow years closed on the locked ward. Since returning.
Ever since you left for college and came back ranting, since you'd let
too many things dissolve on your tongue. Even then I was hoping.
And the night I went looking for the movie listings and found
the newspaper article, North Brunswick Man Shot, I couldn't see
how your brain waves could still shiver across any screen and I was so
selfish — only seeing my own sudden lack of place, since all I'd wanted
to be when I grew up was yours. And when all the gentle voices began
pronouncing the word self-inflicted, those pretty infants of the thorazine
dreams scattered briefly, reconvened when the nurses' station confirmed
you were alive. Since then, since sitting at your bedside and reading aloud,
buttoning your shirts and wheeling you towards the window, since pacing
in the waiting room through your surgeries and lowering my head
with your parents in prayer. Since we did not know how old you would grow,
how long your skull would keep its delicate luck and I wanted the reassurance
of some tiny version of you brightening in my belly. And even after,
when we could be sure you'd live, even since your rehabilitation,
since the years of college dorm rooms with the familiar suitcase in the corner.
Those first accidental chances, when we'd spend the night in a panic

and the morning choosing names. And since then, the recent deliberate
recklessness — you toweling off after the shower, deciding the blue line
of the test kit would be some holy signal for us to marry. We've passed
the children of our families back and forth between us practicing.
I know just what you'll look like, taking a boy from my arms.
At fifteen we said we'd name him *Noah,* which means comfort, and later
He became *Caleb,* which means faith, but now I think let's call him *Jonah,*
the word for dove, the one animal who flew from that arc after forty days
and nights were done — the covenant dove, who carried back an olive branch
as proof of rising land, who found all those raging waters warm and calm.

They've Come a Long Way
From Ten O'Clock Curfew

The night of your twenty-fourth birthday, you have me on the couch
in the basement of your parents' house and while you move
inside of me, I'm thinking about our first date, sitting on opposite ends
of this same sofa with Sadie panting between us. I remember how
she hopped down and peed on the carpet right in front of us
and you didn't run for paper towel and tonic water. You just
rolled up that rug and slid it to the corner. Eight years later, I snicker,
remembering, and you think I'm laughing at the things you're whispering
in my ear. This is the place where you fired the gun and it's hard
to feel sexy. When you leave me tucked under a spare quilt,
it's punishment. You'll sleep two stories above and I will lie on the couch,
trying not to picture your blood on the floor. Before you woke up
in the hospital, your father told me how once you hid a boy in this basement
for two days — In the sixth grade, you invited a buddy over without asking
and when your mom said no, you smuggled him in anyway. They caught you
sneaking down a plate of food and a canteen of grape juice. When I heard it,
I laughed until I cried but back then, I easily cried. And tonight, I'm thinking
about that kid eating cold chicken in his sleeping bag and I recognize
the lengths he has gone for you. I used to hate Sadie because
you walked her right before you did it. You didn't leave a note

for anyone, but you clipped the leash to Sadie's collar and trotted her around the block. Tomorrow morning, your dad will find me down here and shake you awake, shouting that I'm not some dog — I'm allowed on the good furniture. From now on, I'll sleep beside you in your own bed. Your parents won't say a word even when we head upstairs right after dinner and shut the door. At fifteen, I couldn't have imagined it. Maybe I could have pictured you kissing my forehead before heading up the steps — But the rest of it? I couldn't have imagined it at all.

Came Tumbling After

The first morning after this entire world was reduced
to a place you chose to leave, I stand in the shower and swear
that my family will throw in the handfuls of dirt too — If you
are lowered down, I won't let you lay on the earth's colder side
alone. When the chaperones found the suede satchel of weed
in your tuxedo pocket, they sent you home from the prom.
I always knew I should have followed. I'm now eighteen, weigh
eighty-six pounds and know that if I throw myself down
in the tub, I can snap a hip. If you live, I will eat. A flimsy fury
kneeling on the porcelain, sealing her peace treaty with Jesus.

For years, I have remembered that bath that way — the reassuring
razor in my hand, the medicine cabinet stocked with all its possibilities
of relief. I imagined the medics in your basement peeling off
their bloody gloves, the ambulance siren silenced on its desperate
way. Hard bargain made and kept. And so I've grown grateful
to your life for my life, to your surgeon's intricate work
for the spoonfuls of rice I finally let my mouth close around.
The two of us have our favorite hospitals the way some couples
have their favorite restaurants. We have both carried the visitor's pass

importantly, but they strapped me to the bed first. So that now
you accuse me of yanking your ankle, on my way down
that steep and craggy hill. God

no. You lived because the man with the masked mouth made
it happen, because of skills similar to those of the jeweler
leaning over the old woman's slim and silver watch. I brokered
a deal I could keep either way. Clockwork, listen. You so easily
remember the times I was Eurydice, when the ward's locked door
slid closed between us. Do not forget I have also been Orpheus,
on my knees in the boat, asking all the devils for your face in the trees.

Says the Miracle's Woman

It has little to do with actual animal
lust — this habit of clinging to you
in a darkened car in my own driveway.
If I can keep you attached to me,
I can anchor you to the world. Otherwise
something safe, some strongbox
in which your heart beats, feels
disassembled. I know
that in your head stretches a world
paved with ways to die, methods
hunched over in the shadows,
ready to leap into the light
at the slightest misstep.
So in the dark I cover your eyes,
in my hands gathered so many versions
of our story to live.

My sister, a nurse, tells me about
an elderly couple who,
after learning of his Alzheimer's,

planned their double suicide. They decided
on one bullet — They would stand head
to head. He would shoot her
and the bullet would continue through,
killing them both.
When the man pulled the trigger, his wife
crumpled against him and he stood
still waiting for the bullet. And he did not
fire the gun again, but called for help, begged
his wife to live. When attempts to revive her
failed, all he would do was curse her
for not sharing as if it were a certain section
of the newspaper, maybe
the last piece of pound cake.

When I think of you in your basement
with a gun, I imagine ways
I could have been heroic. Sometimes
I can just talk you out of it. Others,
I have to wrestle the gun from your hands.
And since I heard that story, I've been running
towards you, gripping your shoulders and pressing
my forehead to yours. Not because
I'd take the bullet for you but because I know
you would never pull a trigger
anywhere near me.

It turns out I didn't need to save you.
Someone else saved you,
in your basement, in surgery —

102

someone kept saving you. For whatever
reasons — because it was their job
and they knew how. Maybe they had a son
just your age. Or maybe
they saved you for me, forced open your eyes
and knew that somewhere was a girl
who dreamt in that exact shade of blue
and would thank them silently and often.

Driving home from the beach house,
we've spotted the exit too late and suffer
driving by the off-ramp, an eighteen-wheeler
bearing down behind us, gritting our bumper
between his teeth. You say you would have cut off
the truck — Had it not been for me
in the passenger seat you would have risked it.
And yes, I am in the car. We are both safe. But how
can I get out of the car and leave you
behind the wheel when this is the sort of dilemma
you provide every day — *Leave and trust him*
to live. Try to love him well enough
that he'll stay, that he'll drive home as carefully
as a bus driver, an elementary school
bus driver, anyone driving home
anyone treasured.

Reunion

At the picnic of backward glances, I look
for your replica in all the brick corridors,
then beneath those chestnut trees we shook
down for buckeyes, and near the picket lockers
you once pressed me against. That quiet
library is still quiet. The old floorboards
in the Elm Farm schoolhouse slope right, jut
up in perilous spots and the sills are still shored
with wax and felt against rain. The familiar box
of neckties in the front office is labeled
as always — *Honor our dress code.* And all clocks
keep the uniform slow time, the days — stable
and measured by bells that chime the same.
There is the glass case where they keep
the flag each night, etched with the names
of boys killed at war and brass plaques creep
along the walls still. The smell I thought
was yours is not yours, is only the linseed
rubbed into wood, baking soda still caught
in the rugs after the mute janitor has cleaned.

But in dim corners, I see you blurry and beardless
tucking your defiant shirttails again or bent
over a girl crying in the stairwell — You're fearless
in how you love her and she is me. Back then
you stood between me and the world like a mother
stands between her child and the bayonet when
the soldier has lost all reason and mercy. Other
boys were less kind but grew into the men they meant
to become. They're mingling in the garden — contented alum.
I'm back on that staircase, crouched over, numb.
And thickets still shield that river where we hid from
the encroaching world. And you? Well, you have changed some.

It Wasn't From Lack
of Love for the World

Shame on me for how often I have pictured you
sitting cross-legged on the cellar floor, arms
folded to rest on your knees, turning the gun
in your hands until its narrow barrel faces you,
rests above the bridge of your nose, between
your eyes. I have seen you find holiness in the
smallest portions of the world and then console
yourself with that. You, opening a box of
cookies in the supermarket and offering one
to the checkout girl. Swapping magazines
with some toddler at the doctor's office. Gently
teasing the stammering waiter. You have drawn yourself
out of me and cupped your hand over that left spot
with the same tenderness I can see unwrapping
the gun from its shroud of flannel rag. I mean
it only makes sense to believe you held it
with the same cherishing grip — Each new planet
spun in the revolver's chamber, the barrel's modest
distance marking the last length you'd travel
away from us.

The Baby Question, in terms
of the Religious Question

Every evening before riding the deliberate
elevator to that last locked wing on the tenth floor,
I would stop first at the cathedral on George Street
to light a candle at the pietà, that Madonna adoring
the wrecked son gathered in her arms. Fold a dollar
through the iron slot and say Hail Marys, memorize
her porcelain face and arrange mine into a similar composure.
Then I'd go to lean against the metal rail and watch your eyes
blink, check all the hissing machines responsible
for your pulse, those miraculous paddles ready to jolt
you back to us again and I could only be grateful.
You had meant to die and had been refused
so I began to worship a god of complicated mercy.
In the hospital lobby, I broke bread with your family
and the rabbi with my rosary beads hidden in my sleeve.
Then your astonishing awakening, how each day
something worked that we thought would never work —
your left eye hovering, focusing, your carefully monitored
big toe, the growing croak of your voice. And maybe
we all used me as a bribe, the blonde thing hovering

at your bedside, you and I huddled together with
the bed curtains drawn around our shoulders —
You told me your secrets and I told them
to your doctors and then they sent me off to school
with your yearbook picture packed in my trunk.
I did not betray you.

And during the long winter of your talking cure
when I was only another dangerous substance to keep
from you, I spent Christmas Eve in the little shrine
and prayed only that you considered yourself saved
and not failed. And then the answering machine
novenas, those mailbox invocations finally worked
and you stood in the doorway of my college dorm room
with your fierce need and your fading scar — what else
could you have been but risen and risen only for me?
The two of us and our health parade holding fast
against the ghost of your old trigger. Sometimes,
when there is a prize, there is also a consolation
prize and I have rarely been clear which one I am.

But most recently, you loved me and so I agreed
to trade in my family's candles for your family's
candles and have stood beside you in the temple
and listened to you sing in a language I did not understand.
You held the leather book open between us
and shook your head gently when I turned the pages
in the old direction. And then later in the darkened quiet
of your family's home, you have knelt at the bedside
with your clasped hands and your head bent in prayer.

Every night I've slept beside you, it's been just this way.
Either you are thankful or hopeful. Either you have just
been inside me or you will be momentarily — I am stretched
across the down and flannel, offering. Both prayed for
and prayed to. If I told you I felt like Mary facing the angel
of her blessing, you would only remember my insistent
christening gown — the thin eyelet linen, always hanging between us.
Know that when I lose you, I will lose my every gratitude.
Each reason for belief accumulated. And so while you ask
and thank, I lay there. Quietly precious, until I can press
my lucky body against your lucky body, hoping only
that the holy spirit never swims from the room.

Box Seats, Bob Dylan, 1998

While we maneuver the chairs
so we sit as close as possible,
the couple behind us laughs,
then introduces themselves; Nancy
and Tom — They met, he tells us,
at a show almost thirty years ago.
But I couldn't see
past her. I couldn't even say
whether Dylan was actually
on stage that day. And Nancy looks at me
so tenderly, the way women look
at photographs of their younger selves.

Sitting through *Absolutely Sweet Marie,*
I know they see our shy leaning
into each other, before you clasp your arms
around me and rest your chin
on my shoulder, and I can feel the pulse
at your temple blink

against the pulse at my temple.
I can close my eyes and brush you with lashes.
And I don't realize how frantically tangled
we look, until after you leave
to make your way closer to the stage,
and Nancy passes me her binoculars,
asking *Is it the crowd that makes you so*
nervous? Or is it sitting up here, in the balcony?

What do I tell her? It's not the heights
that frighten me. It's the darkness
some heights hang at the edge of.
But I can't tell Nancy how little we have left
to fear. How we've already lived
through our locked wards, our visiting hours,
how we've each lived through the other
not wanting to live. Suddenly, this
is crucial to me — that Nancy never knows
any truth other than the two of us
huddled in the balcony.

Tomorrow, we'll let each other go
like people used to letting each other go.
I'll turn away without watching you
drive off. But when Tom tells this
story, we'll always be the young lovers
who couldn't keep their hands off
each other. I'm the girl who's borrowed
their binoculars to track you through the crowd.
And you're the boy heading for the stage,

not even needing to look back
to know I have one hand pressed
to my face, holding the place
where your cheek was.

Nightmare of Horse and Church

Your blacksmith hands holding me in place, against the crackling
anvil of all our lost potential, your teeth of the jackal but then
the gentle eyelashes lowering against my throat. Your hands, smelling
of gun powder and mine of my own sick. O rosary, o hospital
love. My long fluorescent corridor and your confinement. Thirsty
so I held the drinking straw to your lips and sorry so I marked my own
arms with scars, scars, and months later you stood in my doorway,
trembling. Still need. Months later on your knees in my father's house.
Still. O need, o city of gratitude rising around us, loveless metropolis
of skyscraper pride and trolleys of the lonesome. Our rickety architecture
claims its victims. Boxes of letters have been shredded but I won't wipe
your handprints from the sliding glass door. Your blacksmith hands,
all your cast iron confidence. No wedding or children but we did have our
secrets, our carelessly inflicted affections. O shared affliction. Undiluted
need. *Fine,* you said, *Leave. But I know who you see when you close
your eyes at night*. All our lost potential, our sorry scars. In the post office
of star-crossed lovers, you wink from the sheriff's posters, fugitive.
Come home. Where is my twin ruin, my holy solace? Nothing kneels down
in my tiny life — this cathedral where your face stains the windows.

Her White Flag

What meaning does the word recovery have for you?
     Sick meant asking for less between myself and
     the world. That sullen refusal to self preserve.
    But the world rewards with the helplessness
  prize. You have to measure being priceless
against having power.

Did you see yourself as powerless in your illness?
    I held my entire family hostage
    with my emerging ribcage. But
  slept on the heating grate and still
could not keep myself warm.

Did your restored health help you to feel less exposed?
    The last time I lay beneath him, he turned
    my arm toward the light so that the scars
    glowed. He asked me How do you stand
  to show those to the world, how do you
reach out to strangers and shake hands?

And you interpreted that question as betrayal?
        The skin of a scar is stronger
       than the original, less aware
      of pain. After one quarrel,
     I threw my face into the frame
    of the closed door until my eye
   blackened. Afterwards, he kept
  asking What have you done to
  yourself? Whimpering. So that
 eventually I set the ice pack
against his skin.

Did you feel responsible for the pain your behavior caused him?
    Shocking that when he fired the gun
   I felt nothing. The way I understood
  love, it should have brought me
to my knees.

It sounds as if you believed the two of you were of one body.
    When we were fifteen, I saved everything he'd held
   in his hands: scraps of paper, a plastic toothpick shaped
  like a snowman, the pink stone he'd dropped in my shirt pocket.
 Anything that belonged to Daniel counted as precious. Suddenly
me. First time I tried to leave he swore Never. Half of who I was
was him. This kept me safe from myself finally. But also I bristled.

Why did that particular declaration alarm you?
People also use the word recovery to describe
gathering the shards of the broken.
Divers swimming circles around the
shipwreck and taking.
Meaning: to salvage.

And that was not enough for you?
Every time we came back to each other,
his arms around me felt like the native country.

If that's true, what sense does it make that you are apart?
The two of us can close our eyes and see each other standing
on the highest point of that footbridge arcing across the river.
Looking like we've been raised only on milk and light.
I have lain next to him and listened to him tell me You are
irreplaceable. You are my childhood. One way to ruin a man
is to burn his home. He was the land I grew up on.
And then became the can of gasoline, the match.
Then that burning field.

You could not forgive him?
Each other. Now I only remind him
of his childhood. We could not
forgive each other.

Morning Prayer

When we were fifteen I believed I could ask God for you
in the same spirit as the Catholic school basketball team,
making the sign of the cross before every foul shot. As if
I could earn you with unashamed faith and the sheer
frequency of my asking. That summer, I sent you letters
from London on the handkerchief airmail paper and bent
at each visited shrine to the sternest of saints. Three years,
three sets of birthday candles blown for you. But
you were nowhere; you sang to me over the telephone, you
woke up states and states away. You believed someone
was poisoning you, that animals prowled in the hair dryer
and so you missed my school play. I wasn't allowed
to bring you to the prom. You were older than me and suddenly
seemed grotesquely younger. You were frailer
than me and the sound of my voice made you chew through
the skin on your hands. And then you lay in the surgical theater,
in the bed in the glass room. Still as a painting
I could visit in a gallery. Each day, before I came to sit
beside you, I stopped at the cathedral behind the train station.
I lit candles with my father's dollars, trying to buy your life

with prayer. Every time a train arrived or left, all the fiery wicks
flickered and I pictured all the hospital's critical wavering too.
Because you lived, I have a heavy debt to God. In the mornings
I wake and try to feel you somewhere in the world. Whole
as the loaf of bread in my hands. As certain as church
and unaware of its angels.

She Attempts the Last Word

On the way to the train station, you told me that every time we left
each other you wondered how we would ever survive it and the last time,
at the Chinese food place, you asked if I would slit my wrists
when you finally drove off with no map back to me creased
in your pocket. Let me tell you now I am no suicide bride. Each morning
I rise and wash and dress and work and think of you only
on the train when I am hurtling from one end of my life
to the other. You don't wait to collect me from those platforms
anymore. The first time I reached for your hand, I did so
through the metal hospital railing, whispering to you under the hum
of all the electricity keeping you alive. Your fingers closed around mine
blindly, the way an infant will grip any finger held within reach
so I won't ever say that you chose me. No one gave you
many choices then. After all, you pulled that trigger
decisively. They put you in a coma so that you would not
move your head. And later you'd look up and see me fixed
in the doorway, over and over, never waiting for your welcome —
But I did see you brighten and then came the days
you'd turn on the light only to see me. If I've kept any piece
hidden from you over these years, it was the secret fear

119

that my love for you hovered at your most desperate moment, hovered
and simply held.

                     At Grand Central Station, I think of you dancing
under that constellation ceiling, spinning across the marble towards
the last train home. I see so many reddish beards and think each time
that you've chased my train with your car, buckle first with relief
and then under the retraction of relief. All of our mistakes — innumerable
as stars. We thought I worshiped you in the pity church. And
in the hospital, holding the drinking straw to your lips, doubtlessly
I loved you. Tenderly. But not nearly so much as these last years
of your telephone songs, of my breath caught in the receiver, the receiver
on the floor — your heroic love singing towards me. How sad for us
that I have made a myth of us when what keeps me from sleeping
is the memory of leaning against you in the bath,
the bar of almond soap in your hands. Or that last morning,
in the quiet between the train's whistle. Your honest back
turned, waiting for me to walk away from you.

How She'll Remember Him

One year after you closed your eyes to the world,
expecting to see nothing more of it than a retreating
light, we race each other through the dune grasses,
running so that our feet won't burn on the sunlit beach.
I am spinning towards the breakers with my arms
raised, my eyes shut. Loving the muscular work
of my legs lifting through the heavy sand.
And I hear you say *Look at you — You are so
happy.* Open my eyes to meet your wet cornered
squint. You're shaking your head because I have
astonished you. Behind us, the Atlantic looks like only
another vast avenue that could have led one of us
away from the other. And didn't.

Three-Minute Celebration of Regret

I give myself three minutes to go back to the prep school
field house, to stand in buckle shoes again with a dickie
under my sweater, the haircut that left half my bangs
soldered to my right eye. Let myself see you coming, how you
slow yourself down to lean next to me against the bleachers.
And when you ask Would you have lunch with me? this time
I let myself hear the wish in your voice, wait for you
to squirm a little. I'm not that stunned bunny, amazed to see
the owl skid down from the sky — I'm so not flabbergasted
this time. Two minutes now to remember how expectantly
you looked at me, how many times you swallowed before
turning to cross the gymnasium with your hands burrowed
in your pockets, the studied shrug tugging your shirttails
out of place. If I call out Wait, it will echo across the court
like a cheer, the referee whistling Foul.

              Later on, after we spend whole
nights on the telephone, my mother will activate the oven
timer when you call. We'll rush in hushed whispers
at the final buzzer. But I have one minute now to convince
myself not to follow. You're headed for the canal and
we're not allowed behind the soccer fields. The tenth grade

ruling class will have something to say about you and me
sneaking off alone in the woods. Internal conflict:
The girl with the bad haircut stands at the half court line.
Even a decade later, after grown men have asked for her
expertly, even after you become someone composed
enough to order her out of her clothes, she'll still consider
her life marked right here and halved with that hard-luck hand.
River picnic. Before she was yours and when. Because of course
she follows and finds you waiting on the field house steps. Now
I'm just one wide eye spying from the rafters. I mean, that's it
for me. I'm out of time.

PUSH YOU ARE HERE.

PURE SUNSHINE BRIAN JAMES

cut
Patricia McCormick

KEROSENE
chris wooding

you
remind
me of
you
a poetry memoir
by eireann corrigan

IN STORES NOW

✳✳✳✳✳✳✳✳✳✳✳✳✳✳✳✳✳✳✳✳✳✳✳✳✳✳

BE A PUSH AUTHOR. WRITE NOW.

Enter the PUSH Novel Contest for a chance to
get your novel published. You don't have to
have written the whole thing — just sample
chapters and an outline. For full details, check
out the contest area on ***www.thisispush.com***

✳✳✳✳✳✳✳✳✳✳✳✳✳✳✳✳✳✳✳✳✳✳✳✳✳✳